The Bridge to Happiness

An Engineer's Approach with 50 Effective Solutions

D0920222

Hans Schols, P. Eng.

Copyright © 2023 Glenelg International Ltd

happiness@glenelgintl.com

ISBN: xxx-x-xxxx-xxxx-x (Paperback)

ISBN: xxx-x-xxxx-xxxx-x (eBook)

Self-Help, Happiness, Habits

Dedicated with Love

To my wife Kimberly and my daughters Erin and Dayna, who have added happiness to my life.

Acknowledgments

Many thanks to my wonderful wife, Kimberly, for all the insight and advice she offered in the writing of this book.

Thanks also to Gary Young for his suggestions and proof reading.

Contents

This book is intended to be read slowly so that you can think and consider how each topic and idea might influence you and your happiness. Resist the temptation to quickly look at all of the topics.

Set aside a few minutes a day to review your happiness plan.

Enjoy the happiness journey - discover how you could be a little bit happier in your life and impact the happiness of others.

There is a table of contents located at the end of the book.

The Bridge to Happiness

Introduction

Everyone is an individual. Everyone is unique. Happiness is something that everyone defines differently. It is important to realize that what makes one person happy does not necessarily make another person happy. For that reason, there is no overall formula for happiness. It is personal. As such, each person will choose different actions to implement in order for them to make an improvement in how happy they feel. The list of actions for each person will be different, and the importance of the actions on the list will also be different for each person.

This short, concise book is about what can make you a little or a lot happier or how to avoid some unhappiness. Only *you* can decide what is important. The book is also very concentrated in that it covers many topics without a lot of verbiage. Unlike other books on happiness that provide stories, examples, and research discussions, this book provides a very short paragraph on each item and leaves it up to you to determine what feels right to you and then to research it further if you feel the topic is important to you. In that way, you get to see the big picture and can focus on yourself. There are many different ways a person can improve their happiness factor. What is important is that you pick those initiatives that fit your personality, your strengths, your culture, your challenges, and your values.

This is also not a 'quick read' book. This book should be read slowly with thought and consideration about what is important to you. If you sincerely wish to find some more happiness in your life, then consider the suggestions in this book, do some research, take notes, personalize it and take action. Find a few minutes a day on weekdays, hopefully at the same time each day, to review your happiness action plan. Ask yourself, "Are you accomplishing what you want to accomplish?"

Nobody is going to tell you what to do, how to do it, or is going to support your initiative while you make changes in your routines or activities. It is completely up to you to make your 'happiness journey' happen and completely up to you to stick with and implement your plan. You are in charge of your own happiness.

A lot of happiness in our lives is all about what we do, what we don't do, and what we think. Some of the suggestions made can be implemented quite quickly, while others take some time to complete. It is suggested that you revisit this book a few times as you implement your chosen happiness factors. Over time you will see life differently, and you might want to implement other ideas. The purpose of the book is to make some small changes in the way you see life and how you feel. These small changes can result in big happiness gains!

WHAT IS HAPPINESS?

Is sitting on a horse considered 'riding'?
Is treading water considered 'swimming'?
What is beauty?
What is nature?

The question "what is happiness?" is difficult to answer. Is happiness a life of pleasure, meaning, gratification, or recognition?

'Vocabulary.com' defines happiness as: *"that feeling that comes over you when you know life is good, and you can't help but smile. It's the opposite of sadness. Happiness is a sense of well-being, joy, or contentment."* The synonyms in Microsoft Word are *"content, pleased, glad, joyful, cheerful, and delighted"*.

Happiness in life can be viewed as having two components. The first component is 'positive emotions' and can be considered more in-the-moment or short-term. Positive emotions can be such things as satisfaction, joy, delight, love, peace, or contentment. The second component is the sense that life is alright, things are looking positive in the future or that life has some meaning or purpose. This is the long-term aspect of happiness. We need both for true happiness, although it must be realized that these components will not always be present. Life has a way of throwing curve balls at all of us, all the time.

Happiness also typically involves mental, physical, emotional, and social health. But 'typical' is not 'you', since 'you' are 'you', and 'you' are 'unique'.

Therefore, the real answer to the question of 'what is happiness' can *ONLY* be answered by *YOU*, the reader. But how *YOU* do that needs to take into account your personality, interests, life, challenges, your past, where you are today and where you want to be in the future. This book provides you with options that can be tailored to suit you.

One important thing to understand up front is that everyone has some sort of struggle that other people do not know about. You might think that certain people have 'perfect lives' and 'are so lucky'. The reality is that no one has a perfect life without dealing with challenges. We have all read about celebrities or 'successful people' that have it all but who reveal hidden struggles or dark moments in their past.

So, if you are struggling, don't add to your burden because you think you are the only person struggling. Everyone has struggles. You are not alone.

One benefit of feeling a little happier is that when the downturns come, as they will, you will be more resilient and better able to avoid negative thoughts. And better able to overcome a challenge. This will allow you to move forward faster and regain that happiness feeling.

There are numerous suggestions of varying degrees of difficulty in this book to choose from that will increase your happiness factor. If you choose to implement your personal choice of the suggestions, you will learn how to make concrete steps towards more happiness.

Being happy is the result of the many, many, many things that you do or don't do on a daily and yearly basis. This means that, to a large extent, you are in control. People rarely spend time thinking, "What should I be doing or not doing in my daily activities to make my life more positive on a macro scale?". The suggestions in this book can lead to a result of both 'being happier' and 'avoiding unhappiness', which means that you are better able to deal with the challenges that always come along, resulting in an overall more positive outlook.

Genetics, past circumstances, marital status, work situation, neighbours, and even the weather can influence how happy you are. Research has shown that your degree of happiness is under your personal control if you focus on it and if you are willing to go through some discomfort at times. For example, changing the nature of some of your relationships may be uncomfortable at first but worth it. In addition, a fair bit of feeling happy is determined by the pursuit of things you want to accomplish, not the end result.

The answer to the question "What is happiness?" is up to you. You decide what makes you 'feel better' or 'happier'.

The goal of this book is to give you some additional thoughts to add to your own thoughts about happiness. As mentioned earlier, this book is also written in a very concentrated way. The purpose of this book is to provide you with ideas that you can then implement, research, or discard. This is about *you* and your choices in life.

SADNESS

As mentioned previously, life will throw you curve balls that you do not want. But that is life, and it is important to know that sadness is part of everyone's life. As you embark on a journey to find more happiness in your life, remember that sadness is also part of life and is something that should also be accepted and dealt with rather than being suppressed. Embrace both happiness and sadness.

Read this book slowly over time

Think about each topic

Pause

Reflect

Enjoy

Be Happy

NOTES

There are note pages throughout the book and also several at the end for you to write down your ideas and actions items.

_____

_____

_____

_____

_____

_____

_____

_____

_____

_____

1.0 The Key Component - You

1.1 Individuality

What makes a person happy or sad depends very much on their personality. The Myers-Briggs Personality Type Indicator is widely used to identify a person's personality type, strengths and preferences. The indicator questionnaire provides insight into the likes, dislikes, strengths and weaknesses of people so that they can lead healthier, happier lives. The four scales of the questionnaire from MBTI (and one extra scale that is sometimes used) are:

Extraversion (E)	Introversion (I)
Sensing (S)	Intuition (N)
Thinking (T)	Feeling (F)
Judging (J)	Perceiving (P)
Assertive (A)	Turbulent (T)

If you go to websites such as 16personalities.com, you can read about the different basic personality types. The first thing for you to do if you have not done it before is to go through the questionnaire and determine your type. Then read about what it says about your personality and determine if you agree or disagree with it.

The website 16personalities.com will also send you updates from time to time on how your personality deals with situations. See if you agree with their comments.

Understanding your personality is important to determine which items in this book are significant to you. Here is an example. Most books on happiness state that 'social interaction' is important. However, social interaction needs to be defined for different personality types. Some people are happy with chit-chat about surface-level topics such as recent news events, sports, or the latest vacation. But other people are interested in talking to people about their thoughts, emotions, and what makes them be or think in a certain way. Social interaction, therefore, means something different to different personality types. It is important to remember that all types of personalities are equal, and no type is better or worse than another type.

Many of the items you will read about in this book are generic and will apply to everyone. Other items will apply more to certain personality types. It is up to you to decide which ones are important to you.

Write down what your personality type is.

_____

_____

_____

1.2 Your Life at the Present Time

Quite a bit of how happy you are depends on what occupies most of your time during the day. If, for example, you go to work every day, are busy raising children, or volunteer at a charity, you may feel a sense of purpose. There are two 'happiness' aspects to being busy in this regard. One is that, hopefully, you feel happy doing what you are doing. The other is that if you don't quite feel happy, then you are still busy and don't have time to dwell on not being happy.

One thing that is evident as a result of the Covid pandemic is that many people changed their lives by either moving out of cities to smaller communities because they could work from home or they switched jobs. This is a great example of how a change affects happiness. The suggestions in this book can build on whatever other changes you are making in your life.

People who retire often struggle with happiness because suddenly they are not busy all day long, whether or not they were happy or unhappy in their work position.

The recommendation in this book is that everyone can benefit from some 'happiness' reflection, no matter how busy or good they feel at the present time, because life is fluid and change is the only constant. By going through some of the exercises in this book, you will be happier tomorrow and more prepared for the future.

Hans Schols

NOTES

Life consists not of holding good cards,

but in playing those, you hold well.

Josh Billings

Hans Schols

NOTES

2.0 Some Basic Solutions

2.1 Smile

Why is 'Smile' number one? It is not easy to smile all the time, but it is completely within your control, and you can do it immediately when you think about it and want to do it. When should you smile? Smile, of course, when you are happy, but also try to smile when you are: unhappy, frustrated, upset, discouraged, aggravated, or annoyed. Remember that the sun comes up every day. Sometimes it is behind the clouds and the rain. Sometimes the sun is there, but you have created your own thunderstorm and cannot see it. Smile while you are trying to sort out your emotions.

Whatever the reason for your displeasure or unhappiness, a smile can relieve your tension and make you realize that whatever is bothering you is perhaps not as big a problem as it seems. You are late for an appointment due to traffic. Smile. There is nothing you can do about it in the present. Relieve the tension. You can only deal with the situation when you get to your destination. It is an opportunity to learn from the experience and leave earlier next time. Listen to music. Drive carefully.

They say it only takes one hour for people to forget to remember to smile. So, write it down 'smile' in several places.

2.2 Be Kind

Don't tailgate. Say thank you. Remember people's birthdays. Do a good deed. Contribute to joint events. Help someone. Pick up garbage.

Kindness is returned by kindness. Kindness makes you happier through reciprocity. Generosity makes you feel good. Be kind without expectations. Be kind because you want to be kind to yourself, to others, and to the world.

If you smile and are kind, you will certainly be happier. Imagine the world if everyone smiled and was kinder.

2.3 Physical Activity

Physical activity is one of the most important contributors toward being happier. Research has shown that it has an incredible positive affect on both your body and your mind. From a body point of view, physical activity can help your:

- √ Heart and cardio strength
- √ Muscle strength
- √ Bone strength
- √ Digestive system
- √ Flexibility
- √ Blood pressure
- √ Weight control
- √ Ability to resist disease

From a mental point of view, it can help your:

√ Sleep
√ Balance
√ Brain health
√ Ability to avoid negative thoughts
√ Memory
√ Confidence
√ Stress reduction

Physical activity is perhaps the most promising non-pharmacological, cost-effective way to feel better both physically and mentally. It obviously does not solve all issues, but it is a fantastic starter. Furthermore, exercise is a distraction from daily activities or worries and can be an opportunity to meet other people.

What is meant by physical activity? It does not have to mean signing up for exercise classes or running around the track. It simply means getting out and doing something that requires some movement for a period of time.
Here are some low-intensity ideas:

o Walking
o Swimming
o Dancing
o Table tennis
o Stretching
o Yoga
o Water aerobics

o Tai chi
o Gardening
o Frisbee
o Housework
o Bowling
o Nature Photography

You can also implement little things like walk a flight of stairs instead of taking the elevator or park the car further away from the door to the mall. The key is to walk for a longer period of time.

Depending on how active you already are, the first step is to talk to your doctor. And as a general rule, always take additional physical activity in very gradual steps.

Keep a log and put a checkmark in your calendar if you exercised that day. Try to do your activity three times a week. It also helps if you find a partner to exercise with, as that will greatly assist you with keeping the routine going. Set a goal for yourself over a period of three months. If you smile, are kind, and exercise, you will be even happier.

2.4 Time for Self

Set aside some leisure, rest, and relaxation time for yourself when you need it. This item is much more important for some personality types than others because some people regenerate themselves with quiet time in order to have more energy. During this time, you could read, listen to music, work on a project, try new makeup, gaze at the stars or fix your bike. This time allows you to get away from the hustle and bustle of everyday life, forget about your 'regular' thoughts, nurture yourself and enjoy your own company.

Having time for yourself will allow you to be in a better place to handle life's challenges. It will give rise to more energy, better and clearer thoughts, and will likely lead to activities that you will enjoy in other parts of your life.

2.5 Nutritional Food

In addition to regular exercise, a balanced, healthy diet will make you feel better. The key is balance. You don't have to exclude eating junk food, but all in moderation. Studies have found that a diet that includes a mix of nutrient-dense whole and minimally processed foods guards against conditions such as Type 2 diabetes, cardiovascular disease and obesity. A Mediterranean diet that is low in saturated fats and sugars has been found to lower the risk of cardiovascular disease and cognitive decline. Be sure to talk to a professional to obtain advice suited to your personal situation.

2.6 Dental Hygiene

This may not be directly related to happiness, but it is proven that daily brushing and flossing with regular dental checkups can avoid cardiovascular issues and add to life expectancy. Similar to eating nutritional food and staying healthy, dental hygiene can help you avoid a life challenge.

2.7 Sleep

Getting enough sleep on a regular basis has been shown to be critical for good mental health and the ability to handle stress.

21

There is a growing body of research that sleep affects many of the cells in our body. The amount of sleep can affect:

- o Mood
- o Memory
- o Energy
- o Stress
- o Appetite
- o Blood pressure
- o Cardiovascular health
- o Social relationships
- o Immunity

It might be six, seven or eight hours – but make sure you are rested and get the sleep that you need. Here are some suggestions to improve your sleep if you are having trouble:

√ Exercise during the day
√ Have a routine for going to bed
√ Sleep in a cool room
√ Have a comfortable mattress and pillow
√ Stay away from caffeine later in the day
√ Reduce sugar, saturated fats, and processed carbohydrates
√ Use mindfulness meditation or music
√ Get up early, and do not nap
√ Try aromatherapy
√ Read a book (paper version)
√ Stay away from the blue light of computer screens which can affect your natural melatonin production
√ Visualize happy situations

2.8 Ethics and Morals

This is a topic for reflection. If you don't live your life according to your own ethics and moral beliefs, then it will lead to stress in your life. Is your behaviour right, decent and proper? There are, of course, times in everyone's life when they 'bend the rules' a little. Know yourself. Know your core values. If you are on the wrong side of your beliefs, then make a plan on how to make a change.

2.9 Posture

The spine is critical for health. It is proven that if you sit up straight and walk with good posture, you will be happier. Furthermore, in today's computer work environment and with so much social media interaction over smart phones, being aware of your posture will avoid back, arm and neck pain. Physical pain can greatly affect your mental well-being. Consider Pilates, yoga or other exercises on a regular basis to help strengthen your core muscles. Your core muscles are those muscles that reside in the area of your belly and the mid and lower back. Another great idea is using a desk that allows you to both stand or sit down while you work.

2.10 Laughter

Laughing releases endorphins. Watch comedy shows, read jokes, act funny, and spend time with friends that enjoy a good time.

2.11 Sing

Not everyone has a good voice, but everyone can sing in the shower if they don't want to sing in public. Some studies have shown that singing results in a better mood, improved attention, reduced contemplation, deeper breathing, relaxation, enhanced social support, cognitive stimulation, and a sense of achievement. Try it!

Action Time

As a gentle start, review the items that you think will increase your happiness level. Write them down on a piece of paper as a reminder, and try them out for a few weeks. Try to develop consistency in a routine before you continue reading the next chapters in the book. These simple initial changes will add a lot to the bigger happiness changes you might want to make in your life.

Topic	I Need More of....
	(choose 2- 4 items)
Smile	
Be Kind	
Exercise	
Time for Self	
Nutritional Food	
Dental Hygiene	
Sleep	
Ethics and Morals	
Posture	
Laughter	
Sing	

Activity Tracker

Week	S	M	T	W	T	F	S
1							
2							
3							
4							
5							
6							
7							
8							

Insert letter below in the days that you implemented one of your new Happiness factors

      S > Smile
      K > Be Kind
      A > Physical Activity
      T > Time for Self
      F > Nutritional Food
      D > Dental Hygiene
      Z > Sleep
      E > Ethics and Morals
      P > Posture
      L > Laugh
      G > Sing

NOTES

_____

_____

_____

_____

_____

_____

_____

_____

_____

_____

_____

_____

Don't go through life.

Grow through life.

Eric Butterworth

3.0 Important Principles

3.1 Hedonic Adaptation

These are two big words, but they mean:

'we get bored with what we have'.

The new toy, the new house, the bigger salary or the new fancy sports car all produce temporary spikes in pleasure or happiness, but we quickly become used to these things and return to our previous level of happiness. This is an amazing and critical principle to understand. It is so important that it really should be taught in schools.

There is, of course, nothing wrong with making more money or getting something new. What is important to realize is that if you are unhappy, more money and more toys will temporarily provide a period of happiness, but you will eventually return to your previous level of happiness or unhappiness.

Therefore, if you want to sustain and increase your well-being, you must forget about your genes, status or wealth and focus on your chosen activities, thoughts, and behaviours. It is not where you live or what you accumulate that matters; it is what you do, how you act, and what you think that makes all the difference.

3.2 You Are Not Alone

As you continue reading this book, it is really important to realize and remember that:

1) everyone wants to be happier

2) nobody can be happy all the time

3) everyone has visible and secret struggles

4) everyone has different needs and wants

5) everybody pretends they are happier than they are

6) nobody is perfect

7) everyone is fallible

8) everyone fails and has setbacks when they try new things

Happiness is not something that you directly pursue – it is the result of what happens when you try to accomplish, fail or succeed at initiatives and the way you control your thoughts. Try those items in this book that suit you personally. Don't criticize yourself. Enjoy the journey of discovery, whether it results in success or disappointment and trying something new. Remember that you are not alone.

3.3 Everyone Has a Gift

It is important to realize that everyone has a special gift. It might be athletic or artistic, or something like being a good listener, being empathetic, being friendly to people, being a good cook, having good organizational skills, or having an eye for photography. Write down what you think your gifts are. You might want to come back to this section later as you think of other gifts that you have.

_____

_____

_____

3.4 Failure Is Learning

Most people hate failure. Everyone wants to succeed. Stories about successful people are often in the news. What is often not discussed is that successful people often fail many times before they become successful. Failure is part of the process of achieving something. It is part of learning. If you don't fail, you won't succeed.

Walt Disney was fired from a newspaper because his editor felt he "lacked imagination and did not have good ideas". J.K. Rowling was divorced, supporting a child and on welfare when the twelve largest publishers rejected her first Harry Potter manuscript. One of Oprah Winfrey's first jobs in television ended abruptly after the producer declared she was "unfit for television".

These three people were probably very disappointed or devastated that they failed, but they persevered, fought their disappointment and carried on.

Failure is a big part of life and a huge part of learning about life. It is often said that:

○ Failure builds character

○ Failure provides you with more understanding of a subject or situation

○ Failure builds sympathy, kindness, consideration, empathy, care

○ Failure builds resilience

○ Failure develops your creativity as you learn a new road to achieve your goal

Thomas Edison said, "The way to succeed is to double your failure rate". Henry Ford said, "Failure is the opportunity to begin again more intelligently". When you fail at something, whether it be big or small, you learn about yourself, and that is extremely valuable.

3.5 Activation Energy

A candle has a fixed amount of potential energy in the form of wax that can be burned. To use up that energy-producing light and heat, the candle needs to be lit with a lighter. The energy used by the person clicking the lighter and the resultant flame is called the activation energy. After the candle is burned for an hour, it has less potential energy since there is less wax.

The same is true for implementing any initiative in your life and the suggestions in this book. There is a certain amount of physical and/or mental energy necessary to implement a new positive routine before that routine becomes part of your everyday life. With more positive routines and activities in your life, the easier your life will be because you will feel better, have a better approach to life and will probably not be dealing with as many negative situations. As a result, the daily effort/stress that you have will decrease, directly translating into increased happiness. For this reason, it is important to persevere when trying new initiatives. This relationship is shown graphically on the next page.

There are some things to learn from the fact that activation energy is required to make a change.

1. The easier the initiative is to implement, the lower the activation energy. As you make decisions on what initiatives to implement, keep this rule in mind.

Implementation Activation Energy and Happiness

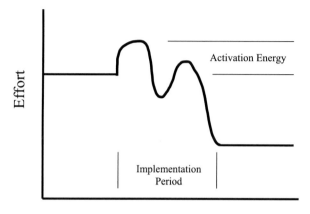

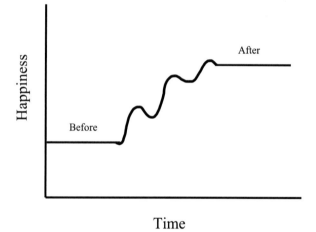

2. Easy initiatives are not necessarily correlated to a lower increase in your happiness factor.

3. Don't take on too many initiatives at once because activation energies are accumulative. Ensure you are successful at your previous initiatives before adding on another initiative.

4. If a large activation energy is required to implement an initiative, then look carefully at your ability to spend that energy. If you can start at a time period in your life where you have the time and energy to make the change. There may be times, though, when you really need to take on another initiative. If that is the case, what is remarkable is that people will often find the necessary time to take on a new initiative.

5. You can change the activation energy. A good example is exercising with a friend. If you do not feel like going for a walk one day, but you know your friend is looking forward to it, you will likely go for a walk.

6. As shown in the diagram, most initiatives have more than one bump in activation energy (AE). Take art for an example. The first AE is to decide what sort of art you are going to do. The next AE is to buy the materials. Then there is the AE to decide on the room to do the art, doing the art for the first time, not being happy with the result and researching how to execute it better, and trying again. You get the point. Be aware

that some initiatives are more complex to take on than others, but they might also lead to increased happiness.

Remember that failure is learning. If you are unsuccessful in getting over an activation energy curve, then try again or try something different. But keep trying!

NOTES

_____

_____

_____

_____

_____

_____

_____

_____

_____

Be happy for this moment.

This moment is your life.

Omar Khayyam

NOTES

4.0 Satisfaction Equation

4.1 Making Lists

Almost everyone is a procrastinator to some degree. We will all put off something because it is boring or hard to do, we are lazy or have anxiety about doing it, or because we incorrectly think we will do it tomorrow. Lists are a great way to accomplish your daily, weekly, or monthly tasks and feel good about them. When a person strikes an item off the list, it feels good, and it releases endorphins. If you strike items off the list, they will be completed, and you will not have the stress of having to do something at the last minute. A good example is buying a birthday gift a month before someone's birthday instead of rushing around at the last moment. Making lists and putting a line through the accomplished items is a 'happy maker'!

There are several ways to do lists. Possible categories are:

i. To do today
ii. Personal items – short term
iii. Personal items – long term
iv. Business projects – short term
v. Business projects – long term
vi. Things to research

Write these lists on two pieces of paper; one for 'to do today' and one for everything else. Keep them in a specific place. Don't do it on a computer. Cross out the item when it is complete. This creates satisfaction! Rewrite the lists from time to time. If an item has been on the list too long, either get rid of it or transfer it to the 'today' list to get it started.

Take a good look at the lists. Is there a balance? Are you overcommitted? Are you doing things at the last moment and getting stressed, or in advance and reducing stress? If an item is a huge project, then add a qualifier to do a component and make a step-by-step plan.

What will lists achieve? They will reduce stress, increase the balance in your life, make you more aware of your daily activities, allow you to focus on the higher priority items, increase your achievement level and make you feel great when you cross out items.

4.2 Variety Is the Spice of Life

By simply changing the frequency and intensity of certain pleasurable activities, we can slow down or halt our hedonic adaptation to them. In other words – change things up! Don't drive the same route to work, try a different type of meal, go to an activity like a concert or play that you normally would not go to, research something new or talk to someone you have not talked to. In this way, you will discover new interests, and the drudgery of doing the same things will pass.

4.3 Memory Makers

A 'memory maker' is an activity or something that you will remember many years later. Think about the positive events in your life that occurred five or ten years ago. Ones that make you say, 'Wow, that was a lot of fun, exciting or memorable'. Usually, there are only one or two of these events a year that our minds remember years later. So, try something different this year and create a memory maker!

4.4 Trying to Achieve Something

It is well known that 'instances' of being happy, for example, getting a new cell phone, receiving a promotion, or taking a vacation, give you a sudden rush of happiness and enjoyment. It is also proven, as previously stated, that these one-time occasions do not lead to continual satisfaction or happiness.

A lot of happiness can come from trying to achieve something that involves some effort, courage, change or complexity. It can be small or big, short-term or long-term.

True achievement involves the many, many steps that you accomplish along the road of trying to get to one's goal, whether or not you actually achieve that goal. It could be learning to be better at something or accomplishing a challenge such as art, coaching, charity work, knitting, teaching, making presentations, hair styling, listening, being empathetic, being organized, time management, eating healthy, exercising regularly, or being grateful. The key is to identify the goal and to be aware of your successes and failures. And if you do not succeed, then you will have learned something about yourself, have the satisfaction that you tried and can move on to another project or goal.

Isaac Asimov, the American writer and professor of biochemistry, said, "The true delight is in the finding, rather than the knowing". The path is more important than the end result.

Achievement can also be looked at in terms of levels. It is natural to choose 'projects' or 'battles' that are simpler to fight. It is the same as looking at a 'to-do' list and always choosing to do the easy items. The sense of satisfaction is not the same. As you think about your goals, think about slowly making them bigger and challenging yourself from an inner perspective. Remember that it is what you learn during this experience that is important and you adjust and respond to 'bumps in the road'.

4.5 Commitment

So far, a lot of suggestions have been made. How are you doing with them? Are you able to choose and implement some of them? Time, activation energy and adapting to change are always hurdles to starting a new routine. Give yourself credit for the things that you have implemented, and remember that making a change in your happiness is a journey that takes time.

If necessary, spend a few minutes thinking about what you want to achieve and write down the action items on a piece of paper and place it somewhere that is visible to you on a daily basis.

4.6 Satisfaction Summary

Here is a list ranking the components of your satisfaction equation:

1) Making lists of everyday items to accomplish

2) Making lists of larger, long-term items

3) Spending more time on some activity that you enjoy, expanding your creativity and seeing where it leads next.

4) Doing something unique that becomes a memory maker.

5) Working on an 'Achievement' project requires some perseverance, effort, courage, or complexity. Happiness comes from working on the project, and it is a bonus if it is successful or completed.

6) Working on a 'Passion' project. These projects are ones that come from the soul, that are 'you', embodying love and desire. This topic is discussed later.

Hans Schols

NOTES

Activity Tracker

Week	S	M	T	W	T	F	S
1							
2							
3							
4							
5							
6							
7							
8							

Insert letter below in the days that you implemented one of your new Happiness Factors

L > Did an item on a List
R > Did some Research
V > Had some Variety in a Routine
G > Worked toward a Goal
P > Worked on something Passionate
M > Thought of a possible memory maker

For every minute you are angry

you lose sixty seconds of happiness.

Ralph Waldo Emerson

5.0 Thankfulness Equation

5.1 Gratitude for What You Have

Are you grateful for what you have? A woman walks down the street to buy some groceries, and she sees another riding a bicycle, and she is envious. But the woman on the bike is envious of the person driving a Chevrolet, who is envious of the person driving a Lexus, who is envious of the person who has a.........

Imagine raising children in a culture in which gratitude is the first priority. Expressing gratitude might seem unimportant and unnecessary, but it is a powerful idea in our society because contentment is often not valued enough. Contentment is a form of happiness, and contentment comes from appreciating what we already have. There is a powerful Thanksgiving Address by the Haudenosaunee (Iroquois Six Nations). It reflects their relationship of giving thanks for life and the world around them. It is an ancient message of peace and appreciation of Mother Earth and her inhabitants.

Be grateful for what you have. Think about gratitude more often. It will make you appreciative of what you have while you work toward other things. When you arrive home, take a period of three minutes once a week to think about what you are grateful for. Or maybe write in a gratitude journal. Or thank someone for their kindness in a card rather than an email.

Studies have shown that gratitude can have a very positive effect on a person's well-being, including improved mental health, becoming unshackled from toxic emotions, using fewer negative words, being more generous and compassionate and feeling less lonely. Studies also noted that these improvements do take time to develop. This fact is true for many of the suggestions in this book because you need to do an activity for a few weeks, months or more before results start showing. Be patient, and the rewards will come.

5.2 Being Grateful for the Actions of Others

Being grateful, thankful, and appreciative is so important, yet all of us forget about it too often. Being grateful means that you have taken action, specifically that you have shown your appreciation to a person that did something for you. This means that you took the time to talk to them, send them a card, an email, a text, some flowers, or acknowledge their action in some way.

Why does this increase your happiness? It is because you will feel that you were kind and appreciative to another person, which is a good feeling, and secondly, the other person will have a good feeling and will be more likely to reciprocate by doing something nice for you. When someone does something nice for us, we feel happier.

5.3 Be Happy for Others

Sometimes it is really hard to be happy for someone when they achieve something that you hoped to achieve. But if you are happy for them, truly happy for them, then it will subconsciously open up your opportunities even more since being happy for others shifts the way you look at things. Happiness for another's success can increase your own happiness because it replaces a negative emotion with a positive one.

When there is a competition, and we don't succeed, are we happy for the winner? We should be; they excelled. Are we grateful that we had the opportunity to compete? It is understandable that you would also be sad or disappointed if you did not win, but ensure that there is a balance between your sadness and your earnest congratulations to the winner. There is always the possibility that you will have your own success in the future. 'The success of one does not diminish the other'.

It has been proven that envy, jealousy, resentment and fear all contribute to inflammation and a higher risk of illness, while abundance, happiness, positivity, hope, and curiosity lead to a sense of well-being and improved health.

It is much easier to be happy for others if you are happy with yourself. Be happy for both yourself and for others.

Life is a mirror and will reflect

back to the thinker

what he thinks about it.

Ernest Holmes

Activity Tracker

Week	S	M	T	W	T	F	S
1							
2							
3							
4							
5							
6							
7							
8							

Insert letter below in the days that you implemented one of your new Happiness factors

      G > Had Gratitude for things in my life

      R > Showed Gratefulness through Action

      H > Happy for someone else

Hans Schols

NOTES

6.0 Happiness Catalysts

This section includes a few suggestions that you can do to quiet the mind or express your emotions. This will result in an increase in happiness.

6.1 Relaxation Techniques

By taking up a relaxation technique such as yoga, meditation or deep breathing, your stress levels will decrease, and your mind will become calmer and clearer. There are many programs that you can stream free of charge on your mobile phone or TV.

6.2 Journaling

A journal is useful for noting both positive and negative experiences or thoughts. Keep a journal of things that you are grateful for, what made you happy that day, what you accomplished, and the positive things in the world around you. Realize that you are fortunate and have many gifts in your life.

You could also record the stressors in your life and the way you dealt with them or did not deal with them. Is there a pattern? Is there a successful way that you dealt with a stressful situation in the past that can be used again? How did you feel physically and emotionally? What did you do to make yourself feel better?

6.3 Exercise - A Repeat

Enough cannot be said about exercise. Use it to your advantage. Use it to clear the mind and to get away. Walking has been proven to be one of the best exercises. Vary the walk as well. Drive to a new location five minutes from where you live and go for a walk there. Daily exercise of some sort is a great happiness maker! It really does help your mental, physical and emotional well-being, and if you walk with someone else, it adds a social component as well. Choose a physical exercise and enjoy it! Here are some other ideas:

- o Lawn darts
- o Bean bag toss
- o Workout videos
- o Pickleball

- o Croquet
- o Bocce ball
- o Bike riding
- o Hiking

6.4 Music

Listening to or playing music can be a quick way to increase your feeling of happiness. Let the good times roll! Listen to music in your house, in your car, at work on your earbuds or blast it out somewhere private. Any time can be music time.

6.5 Nature

The word 'nature' is derived from the Latin word 'natura', which means 'birth'. It is not surprising, then, that a walk in nature is one of the best ways to regenerate yourself. There is preliminary scientific evidence that being in nature has an impact on our brains and our behaviour, helping us to reduce stress while increasing our creativity and ability to socialize.

6.6 Long View

It has been shown that people find it comforting and relaxing if they can see a long view over water, the city, or fields. Perhaps it is the feeling of amazement about the size of the earth. Whatever it is about a long view, find a place, even in a city, that provides you with a distant sightline.

6.7 Find Beauty in the Everyday

Slow down. Don't rush. Take the time to look around at nature, the architecture of buildings, the details in artwork, the designs in clouds, or simply the beauty of the people around you.

6.8 Art

Doing artwork is an amazing way to have fun, destress and let your mind focus on something new. You do not have to be an artist to try this technique because it is the experience of creating something new that is the focus. Buy a water colour set (brush, paints, and paper) and make a small abstract painting. See how the colours bleed into each other. Learn how to improve some new techniques. Try other mediums or types of paintings like landscapes, botanicals, or people. Enjoy the experience.

6.9 Have Variety - A Repeat

A great way to feel better is to simply do something different. It can give you a feeling of 'wonder' or 'wow'. No matter what you see or feel, it will give you a new feeling or emotion. Try going to a different store, using a different recipe, getting up early to see the sunrise, staying up late to see the Perseid meteor shower, or driving down a different street.

Have a goal of doing something unique once a month or more often.

6.10 Time for Self - A Repeat

Take time for yourself when you need it.

6.11 Reiki

Reiki is a form of energy healing that was developed by a Japanese Monk around 1900. Reiki means 'universal life energy' and is based on the belief that there is an energy or life force that flows through everyone and everything. Its practitioners believe that when energy becomes blocked or imbalanced, it can lead to physical and mental health difficulties. By rebalancing the energy fields around the body, a person's health can improve.

6.12 Less Smart Phone Use

If you are the type of person that is always connected to your cell phone, try to give yourself a break. Don't respond immediately to every email or social media post. Don't engage in social media for two, three, or four hours during the day, or put it on silent for two hours in the evening.

Also, realize that, for the most part, posts on social media portray a fake sense of reality that is either too positive or too negative.

6.13 Pets

Having a pet provides companionship, makes you laugh, inspires exercise and is known to reduce stress. At the same time, having a pet is not for everyone since it is a huge responsibility that can affect your lifestyle and be a financial responsibility. If this is something you are interested in and you do not currently have a pet, maybe you can help another person take care of their pet. If you are interested in obtaining a pet, be sure to talk to pet owners about the responsibility before proceeding.

Action Time

Topic	I Need More of.... (choose 2- 4 items)
Relaxation Techniques	
Journaling	
Exercise	
Music	
Nature	
Long View	
Find Beauty	
Art	
Change the Situation	
Time for Self	
Reiki	
Less Smart Phone Use	
Pets	

At this point, remember that making a small improvement in your happiness is a journey, not instantaneous gratification. You will not immediately feel a change in how happy your feel. It will take a while. Change is a journey, an expedition, a trip, a voyage. Like most things in life, you only get better at something with time, knowledge, experience and knowing yourself. Enjoy the journey without expectations and then one day, look back on what you accomplished.

Activity Tracker

Week	S	M	T	W	T	F	S
1							
2							
3							
4							
5							
6							
7							
8							

Insert letter below in the days that you implemented one of your new Happiness factors

> T > Use a Relaxation Technique
> J > Journal
> E > Exercise
> M > Listen to Music
> N > Walk in Nature
> C > See a Long View
> B > See Beauty in the Everyday
> A > Play with Art
> V > Had Variety in my Routine
> S > Take Time for Self
> R > Try Reiki
> L > Use Smart Phone Less
> P > Interact with a Pet

Hans Schols

NOTES

Life isn't about finding yourself.

Life is about creating yourself.

George Bernard Shaw

7.0 The Fun Equation

At the beginning of the book a viewpoint of happiness was stated along with the truth that happiness can only be defined by the individual. To repeat it, the first component is 'positive emotions' and can be considered more in-the-moment or short-term. Positive emotions can be such things as satisfaction, joy, delight, love, peace, or contentment. The second component is the sense that life is alright, that things are looking positive in the future or that life has a purpose or meaning. This is the long-term aspect of happiness.

Where does fun come into the equation? Having fun can either be short term or long term in nature. Short term fun (FUNST) can be things already discussed such as physical activity, playing a sport, singing, playing music, going for a walk in nature, doing art, knitting, or other things like playing a board game, getting together with friends for a good laugh, taking a course, watching a big game on TV, carving pumpkins at Halloween, taking a vacation or going to a movie. Fun activities are also accumulative.

FUNST = SHORT TERM HAPPINESS

FUNST + FUNST + FUNST = MEDIUM TERM HAPPINESS

The great thing is that medium term happiness can than lead to greater things such as the willingness to make positive changes in your life toward greater happiness.

MEDIUM TERM HAPPINESS = MOTIVATION

MOTIVATION = POSITIVE CHANGE

This means that short term fun activities are an important part of the overall happiness journey because it will give you the energy to find or work on a passionate project, avoid activities that lead to unhappiness, and other things discussed later in this book. The long term aspect of fun (FUN^{LT}) is the fun you have enjoying the winding, bumpy road of having a good reason to get out of bed most mornings because you have a feeling of purpose or meaning and that life is ok. (The word 'most' is used because as everyone knows, everyone has good and bad days). For the time being, let's leave the equation at:

HAPPINESS=FUN^{ST} + FUN^{LT} + AVOIDING UNHAPPINESS

The one caution is that some people can use short term fun in the extreme to escape moving to the motivation stage and make an effort to work on more difficult items.

FUN^{ST} X 5 = MEDIUM TERM HAPPINESS

FUN^{ST} X 25 = ESCAPISM

But then, as initially stated, if you are truly, truly happy enjoying lots and lots of short term fun, then that is your choice and it's ok.

8.0 Integration of Time

Albert Einstein once said "People like us who believe in physics know that the distinction between past, present and future is only a stubbornly persistent illusion". Physics also states that time cannot be created. People however, can create 'more valuable time' because it is an illusion that you do not have the time for more valuable activities in your life.

This is fantastic because it means that you do not have to give up your current activities to pursue new ones. Many people often experience this when they manage to squeeze in an education course while working or suddenly have extra family responsibilities during some type of emergency. As a result, you have the time resource to experiment with various short term and long term fun activities. Don't think to yourself 'How am I going to squeeze in a new activity?" Focus on identifying the things that you want to experience, and you will find that you will suddenly have the time to do them.

Time flies when you are having fun.

Albert Einstein

9.0 Other 'Happy' Words

Here is a list of words related to the word 'happy'. Circle or write down the three words that describe you and then three words that you could improve on. For example, perhaps you are currently 'interested' in a lot of things but wish you were more 'confident' doing certain things. Keep these items in mind as you progress in the book.

o Playful	o Valued
o Cheeky	o Powerful
o Content	o Courageous
o Free	o Creative
o Joyful	o Peaceful
o Interested	o Loving
o Curious	o Thankful
o Inquisitive	o Trusting
o Proud	o Sensitive
o Successful	o Intimate
o Confident	o Optimistic
o Respected	o Hopeful
o Pleased	o Inspired
o Cheerful	o Glad

- o For the long term, life is:
  - o on the upswing
  - o alright, ok
  - o looking good
  - o moving forward

10.0 Relationship Components

8.1 Social Interactions

Connecting with others is a natural thing to do for humans, but the ease of 'connecting' can vary greatly depending on whether you are an introvert, extrovert, sensitive person or have anxiety. Therefore, the number of people you connect with or spend time with will depend on you as an individual. What is important is to connect with people when that connection feels like it is in 'balance' for you. You will want to find people who will both share their experiences and listen to your experiences, people who tend to be more positive in their outlook on life, and people who are not always complaining. Relationships are never easy, straightforward, or 'even'. They take work, meaning that both parties need to put in 75% of the effort!

As stated in Section 1.0 on Individuality, different personality types will have different needs and goals when it comes to social interactions. It is important to seek out the correct type of social interaction that suits you. This may be easy for the person seeking the 'normal, chit-chat' type interaction but might be quite difficult to find for those interested in more meaningful, in-depth interactions. Valuable social interaction can lead to a lot of happiness, but at the same time, it can also lead to unhappiness if the person you are interacting with is not pleasant, unhappy, or is not meeting your needs. In the latter case, it is best to minimize contact with them if possible.

Studies have shown that some social interaction has multiple health benefits, such as:

o Increased physical health
o A boosted immune system
o Better mental acuity
o A longer life
o A sense of belonging

Maintaining relationships is usually not an issue for younger people, but as people age or move, they can find themselves more isolated and lonelier. Here are some activities if you want to increase your social interaction time:

√ Volunteering
√ Join a new club
√ Coffee time
√ Movie nights
√ Hiking
√ Video games
√ Card games
√ Concerts
√ Escape rooms

√ Group walks
√ Book clubs
√ Art gallery trips
√ A new class
√ Paint nights
√ Gardening clubs
√ Photography clubs
√ Fishing clubs

Remember to be sure to meet your needs in terms of the type of interaction you want.

8.2 Friendship and Love

Friendships come in different forms and can be complicated, challenging, meaningful, and/or warm-hearted. Friendships can also go through different levels of openness or interaction, both positive and negative. Remember that all people have struggles, are usually dysfunctional in some way or another, have unique preferences and that relationships will change from time to time depending on each person's own circumstances and challenges.

One way to categorize friends is as follows:

- Level 1: People you know that you might meet on a frequent basis for some event but you only interact with them in a superficial way. You might have a lot of fun with these people, but they are not close to you in a personal way.

- Level 2: People with whom you share some basic personal experiences and emotions but in a cautious way.

- Level 3: People with whom you can share more personal stories; those people you feel have been as kind to you as you have been to them over an extended period of time

- Level 4: With these friends, you can share almost everything; you trust them implicitly, they have your back, and you have known them for a long time. These friends are rare.

From a happiness perspective, it is good to have friends at all of the above levels in varying degrees, depending on your personality type. What is perhaps more important is to ensure that you associate with friends that are happy. You will be happier if you are connected with people that are happy.

It is normal behaviour to complain about things from time to time. There is a balance, though. Interact with positive people – people that enjoy life, enjoy nature, enjoy the arts, help other people, like their work, do interesting things, and have an upbeat attitude to the future. Hanging around with negative people will simply bring you down as well.

The takeaway from this subject is to have a variety of friends and to focus on being with friends that are also happy. Remember that friends can also mess up because of their own circumstances at times. If you focus on happiness, you will be more likely to find happier friends and increase your success at love as well if that is a goal. But remember, "To have a friend, you have to be a friend".

8.3 Positive Conversation

If you can't say something nice, don't say it at all.

Compliment other people and minimize complaining about other people, situations, or events. That is not to say that you should never be negative but minimize it. You will be happier, and other people will enjoy interacting with you more.

NOTES

_____

_____

_____

_____

_____

_____

_____

_____

The thing everyone should realize is that

the key to happiness is

being happy by yourself and for yourself.

Ellen DeGeneres

9.0 Why Initiatives Work

Without going into detail, chemical messengers in our body, such as neurotransmitters and hormones, are produced in reaction to things that we do, which in turn makes us feel a certain way. There are many types of happiness messengers, but the four big ones are dopamine, serotonin, endorphin, and oxytocin. A smile releases the first three neurotransmitters. Even a fake smile will be successful in releasing neurotransmitters!

You might ask yourself, "Why should I make a list of things to do? Why should I go out for a walk? Why should I try meditating? Why should I give someone a hug? Why should I eat healthier?"

The answer is simple. If you do these things, the neurotransmitters and hormones in your body will react, impacting your happiness, pleasure, satisfaction, optimism and memory and reducing your level of stress, negative thoughts and feeling of pain. The more positive actions you take, the more you will feel happier.

One interesting fact is that these chemical 'happiness' messengers decrease over time after something positive has happened. As a result, you need to take another positive action to release more messengers. It is one little thing, added to another little thing, that you do every day, every week, every month that makes you feel happy.

NOTES

10.0 Solutions to Unhappiness

The focus so far has been on being happy. This next part deals with staying away from or dealing with the negative influences on happiness.

10.1 Minimizing Public Negativity

Newspapers, television news, some social media, radio news and other media outlets love disasters, crime, murders, and other negative news. Try to minimize this negative news as much as possible.

10.2 Negative People

Temple Grandin, an inventor and professor of animal science, said, "Engineering is easy – it's the people's problems that are hard". There are several types of negative people:

a) 'It can't be done': These people have a glass-half-empty outlook on possibilities. Here is an example of a strategy to avoid these people: A company has to let go of ten employees by giving them a month's notice. Two of the fired people feel very positive about the opportunity to find a better position. Others are negative about the future. The two positive people encourage each other and take their breaks and lunches together to support each other. Those two people found a new job.

b) 'Bad News Spreaders': These people listen to the news a lot and then like to tell others about bad news or disasters. Whether, for example, it is an accident, natural catastrophe or murder, these people are the first to tell others the bad things that are happening in the world, even if it is something that happened on the other side of the globe.

c) 'Grumblers': These people like to grumble about 'something'. The internet is slow; the weather is too hot or cold; the store does not have enough choices, and the traffic is terrible.

If you can recognize these people, then you can either a) stay away from them, b) find more positive people to be with, or c) if you are with a person like that, then change the topic of conversation at the earliest moment to a more positive topic. Awareness of these traits in other people will also make you more aware of yourself.

What is the strategy here to avoid unhappiness?

- Try not to be negative yourself. Positive talk leads to positive feelings

- If another person is negative, try to change the topic of the conversation

- Avoid or minimize time with people who are negative

10.3 Unappreciative People

We all make mistakes and forget to say thank you, forget to recognize that someone did something nice for us, forget to return a favour or forget to appreciate the needs of others. We need to remember that others will also make mistakes. There are, however, people that are much more prone to being unthankful, unappreciative, ungrateful or unmindful.

Interactions with all types of people is part of life, and their thoughts and actions will affect you. Many of these interactions will be positive, but how does one deal with these unthoughtful comments and messages?

It is important to realize that 1) we all have our own issues and dysfunctionalities, 2) their comments or lack of comments to you are not personally directed at you - they treat almost all people that way, and 3) they are acting out their own beliefs and emotions - they are trying to survive in their world.

To deal with these people, try to think of it visually as literally putting the person in their own "Issues Box". In other words, the person you are interacting with has their own issues and is in their own "Issues Box" that has nothing to do with you. You are wise not to let their problems become yours.

If you work hard at something for another person, and they do not thank you, remember that you did a good deed and helped another and that their lack of appreciation is their loss and is not directed at you. It is their lack of mindfulness.

Surround yourself only with people

who are going to lift you higher.

Oprah Winfrey

If a person's behaviour is consistently unappreciative, then perhaps minimize your time with them. If this happens with someone that you need to interact with often, then visually, in your mind, put them in their own "Issues Box" where they are dealing with their own 'stuff'.

People who commit a crime are mean. People with a lot of jealousy may be mean toward certain people. But on the whole, very few people are truly mean, and when we think of a person as being mean, they are really just inconsiderate, unthoughtful or lack empathy because they have their own issues. As an example, if a person says something nasty such as "I don't like white cars," forgetting that you have a white car, then remember that it is their lack of mindfulness and is not directed at you. Nobody is perfect. You can deal with inconsiderate people by drawing a 'line in the sand' for behaviours that are totally unacceptable to you. If that 'line in the sand' is crossed, you can take care of yourself and your happiness by talking to the person about how you feel you have been treated and/or avoiding that person.

People usually react to situations more based on their own issues than what you have done and may hurt you in an attempt to avoid their own hurt. Don't let the actions of others dictate how you feel.

10.4 Lower Expectations of Others

It is normal to have expectations, and everyone should have high hopes. Having high hopes, however, can also create problems because when your expectations of others are not met, they can cause disappointment. Even small unmet expectations can create a feeling of disappointment. On the contrary, if you do not expect anything from another person, you can't be disappointed or unhappy.

In situations where you expect something, like, for example, a thank you from a person, perhaps it is better not to have any expectations. This is especially true if you have been disappointed before by the lack of action from that person. Expectations can be an impediment to enjoying your own life.

Take a look at where you can reduce disappointment by lowering your expectations from certain individuals. The other alternative, of course, is to lessen time with those individuals if that is possible.

10.5 Forgiveness

The topic of forgiveness is a huge one and, to some degree, depends on the size of the action that needs to be forgiven. Whether to forgive or not to forgive also depends on how much the action of the other person is affecting you. Not forgiving can cause you anger, hate, resentment, and pain. The interesting thing is that the other person, the perpetrator, goes on with their life without any consequences, but your life and your happiness, however, have been negatively affected.

Forgiveness is not forgetting, but instead, it is taking the view that the person who hurt you will not continue to have power over you and your happiness. You are not going to focus on the pain and the hurt that you received from that person.

And you are not going to focus all of your valuable energy on that person.

If you are the type of person that has trouble forgiving even small infractions, then research this topic more and make a decision on how you can make a move to forgive certain people so that your life is better.

Activity Tracker

Week	S	M	T	W	T	F	S
1							
2							
3							
4							
5							
6							
7							
8							

Insert letter below in the days that you implemented one of your new Happiness Factors

       M > Minimized public negativity
       N > Minimized negative people
       U > Minimized unappreciative people
       L > Lowered my expectations
       F > Forgave people

All the art of living

lies in the fine mingling of

letting go and holding on.

Havelock Ellis

11.0 Affirmation Support

An affirmation is something that you tell yourself on a daily basis in order to change the way you think about a specific situation or action. For example, if you are scared of public speaking, you could tell yourself that "I have the confidence, ability and knowledge to speak to people about an expertise that I have". Affirmations can also be used to say to yourself every morning, "I am going to have a great day no matter what challenges I face because I know I am doing my best". Affirmations can also be framed around the happiness factors in this book.

Depending on the person, it may take from thirty to sixty days to change the subconscious mind if an affirmation is repeated three times a day. An affirmation is also more likely to be effective if you create a positive mental image. Like many things, it takes effort and is not for everyone, but it can be a powerful tool to add to your arsenal of changing your beliefs.

Depending on where you think you are in your journey and life challenges, you might start with an affirmation that you think is within reach rather than an obscure affirmation. An example of this would be to say, 'I will go for a nature walk every Monday', or 'I will do one item on my to-do list every day'. This type of affirmation is one item, is grounded, focuses on skill, and you can visualize yourself doing it. Stay away from mega statements like 'I am beautiful and love myself' because these affirmations usually fail since people don't truly believe these things.

Once you have completed a few of these types of affirmations and have made progress with your goals, you can then move on to less concrete affirmations such as 'I am so proud that my happiness comes from within me and other people do not affect me'. Write these affirmations down and visualize them. Make the affirmation practice a consistent routine and be patient with the process.

NOTES

_____

_____

_____

_____

_____

_____

_____

_____

There are three constants in life…

change, choice, and principles.

Stephen Covey

NOTES

_____

_____

_____

_____

_____

_____

_____

_____

_____

_____

_____

12.0 Start the Day with a Purpose

12.1 Passion

Wikipedia defines passion as a feeling of intense enthusiasm or compelling desire towards someone or something. Passion can range from eager interest in an idea, proposal, or cause, to enthusiastic enjoyment of an interest or activity, to strong attraction, excitement, or emotion towards a person.

What are you passionate about? For some people, the answer is easy. For others, it is difficult. If it is not clear in your mind what the 'passion answer' is, take the time over a month to write down in a journal what your thoughts are. Don't make any judgments or prioritize; just write them down. What are the things that give you pleasure in a happy or meaningful way? What are the things related to those items that have prevented you from realizing those pleasures? Are there barriers that can be overcome to realize the things that you are passionate about?

After a month, look at the list and break it down into categories, things you are doing, not doing, easy to do, hard to do, work or leisure. Put the list away for another month, and then take another look. Do you still feel the same way? Are there other items to add to the list? In the end, you should hopefully come up with one, two or three items that are achievable.

12.2 Vision Board

A vision board is usually a piece of bristle board or cardboard of a reasonable size on which one sticks pictures, magazine clippings, phrases, or words to affirm your goals and dreams. The board aids visualization of your ideas. Vision boards can work if you are prepared to work toward dreams or ideas and you believe in the law of attraction. They assist you in visualizing what you want, and by their absence, you can also easily see what you have not included and what you do not want.

12.3 Intentions and Goals

As a possible alternative, consider making a goal for the future. Goals are focused on the future. Goals are a destination or specific achievement. Try to set a goal for yourself without thinking about how to get there. Once you have determined your goals, you can then set daily activities or intentions to get you to those goals. Four tips for setting actionable goals supported by intentions are:

1. Identify your why.

2. Be clear about what you don't want.

3. Break down the overall goal into baby steps.

4. Make them SMART – specific, measurable, achievable, relevant, and time-bound.

The objective is to clarify what you are most passionate about doing and then make a good plan on how to make progress toward the goal.

NOTES

_____

_____

_____

_____

_____

_____

_____

_____

_____

_____

_____

Happiness is not something readymade.

It comes from your own actions.

Dalai Lama

13.0 Faith and the Golden Rule

Most people have either a certain level of belief in a religion or they do not. If you are so inclined, the association and involvement with religion has been shown to provide many benefits that can enhance your happiness. Some of the benefits include:

√   A community of friendship and support
√   A strong belief that can give you strength in challenging times
√   Adherence to a set of moral and ethical values
√   Volunteering in activities to give you a sense of giving back
√   An understanding that while the world is full of injustice, there is hope
√   Finding an inner peace
√   Being in charge of our own actions

A strong faith can also help you to focus on:

o Kindness	o Honesty
o Charity	o Patience
o Forgiveness	o Respect
o Humour	o Service
o Compassion	o Goodwill

All of these positive aspects of faith support improved health, self-esteem, empathy, peace and, finally, happiness.

The Golden Rule has been around for about 2,500 years and involves the notion of treating others as you would want to be treated. There are many ways of stating this rule, such as:

Do unto others as you would have them do unto you.

Hurt not others in ways that you yourself would find hurtful.

What is hateful to you, do not do to your fellow.

Do not do to others what you know has hurt yourself.

What is the benefit of this golden rule for happiness? If you are kind to people, then hopefully, they will be kind to you. That would make you happy. Also, if you are mean to others, then perhaps they will be mean to you. That would make you unhappy. If you would like a thank-you card when you do something special for another person, then you should write a thank-you card to someone who does something special for you. This action might develop a closer relationship. That would be positive and make you feel a little happier.

This rule does not always result in the other person reciprocating in the same way that you acted because everyone has their own baggage to deal with. But why not practice the Golden Rule and do your part? It is a step in the right direction that will work some of the time, and more importantly, will make you feel good, and that is a Happy Feeling!

14.0 Financial

Financial pressures create a lot of stress and unhappiness. Everyone has them, and they are unavoidable. To avoid some of the stress, make sure you know where your money is being spent, try to have some money for a rainy day, and have an overall plan. Make decisions on prioritizing where to spend your hard-earned cash.

It is generally accepted that above a certain amount of income, your emotional well-being does not increase, but your temporary life satisfaction does. The more money you have, the better you think your life is, but how you feel on a day-to-day basis cannot be improved by having more money. You can buy the car of your dreams, but after a while, hedonic adaptation applies, and that pleasurable feeling goes, and you need to look for something else.

It is great to make more money, but also focus on your daily happiness actions that will not change no matter how much money you make.

Happiness depends upon ourselves.

Aristotle

15.0 Beyond Control

15.1 Things You Cannot Control

We are not in control of a lot of things that are potential sources of stress: the government that gets elected, the amount of plastic garbage, the amount of traffic or the weather tomorrow. We can, however, control how we react to these outcomes. How does one reduce the stress factor of these situations? One answer is to either do something about it or don't think about it all the time.

If you are concerned about the amount of plastic garbage, reduce your own use and stop reading about the problem unless you want to learn more so that you can do something else. If you are concerned about climate change, then either campaign for change or stop focusing on it all the time. Overall, it is okay to complain occasionally, but do not complain all the time and get stressed out. It is also good to be informed, but not to the point where it affects your attitude and health.

As the saying goes, "Accept what you can't change and change what you can't accept".

15.2 Learn to Say No

Know your capabilities, limits, and skills. Say no to others or to yourself to ensure that you have the balance you need to feel good. If you need quiet time for at least thirty minutes every other day, say 'no' to activities that encroach on that time. Be sure that you can handle additional responsibilities if you accept them. If you have too much to do, then back off. That is not to say that pushing yourself from time to time is not good, but balance is a necessity.

15.3 Go Beyond One Step

There are times when there is a serious situation that you want to help improve or correct, but the action resides with another person. This could be helping a family member, a friend, or even a subordinate at work. These situations can be very stressful if the person involved does not take action to correct the issue.

To reduce your stress level, try your best to help the person and if they don't respond and take care of themselves, try again and again. When you feel that you have done absolutely everything you can, go beyond one more time and try again. If you are successful – great! If you are not, you know that you did everything in your power to help the person and can relieve yourself of any stress that you have. Plus, by knowing that you did your best, you can let go and stop 'trying to change something that cannot be changed'.

Activity Tracker

Week	S	M	T	W	T	F	S
1							
2							
3							
4							
5							
6							
7							
8							

Insert letter below in the days that you implemented one of your new Happiness factors

A > Accepted what you cannot change

C > Changed something that you cannot accept

N > Said NO

G > Go Beyond one step

L > Let go of something after you went one
    step 'beyond' to change it

And in the end

it's not the years in your life that count

it's the life in your years.

Abraham Lincoln

16.0 Five-Year Plan

At this point, you have read, considered and thought about the many ways that you could make changes in your life to be happier. One other technique is to make a five-year plan. Many things in life occur in approximately five-year cycles. Look ahead five years and think – what would I like to be doing, or accomplish, or change at that time? Make a separate book for this exercise, and over a few months, write down your thoughts, ideas and dreams.

When you are thinking about what you want, think only of the end result without thinking of how you would get to that end result. Do not think of the progressive steps that would get you to the end result. Do not think of what you want to avoid. Make the vision concrete and real. For example, do not state "I want to live in a nice community". Instead, state something specific like, "I want to live in a small town of less than 25,000 people located near water". To achieve this end result vision, you must really want what you write down.

About two to three months after you have done this, revisit your five-year plan and write down some steps that you can take to get to where you want to be. These steps can then be transcribed onto the list of your short-term intentions and long-term goals. Keep your book in a place where you will come across it from time to time, and you can look at it.

NOTES

17.0 Solution Analysis

At this point, take a moment to reflect on what you have learned and how you are feeling. What areas of your life are going well, and what is not so good?

- Jot down the activities in this book that you have decided to implement. Give yourself a score of 1 to 5 on how well you are doing. Perhaps there is one activity you would like to improve on.

- Jot down how you are doing in general. A possible list might look like this:

  o I am thankful for
  o I need to change
  o I like
  o I avoid
  o I enjoy
  o I am fearful of
  o I am sad about
  o I exercise on
  o I am angry about
  o I pretend that
  o I love
  o My daily pleasure is
  o I want to change my attitude about

Remember that change takes time, so you will have items on the list that are perhaps discouraging, but don't be discouraged. Reflect on the things that are important to you to make that incremental improvement in your happiness. Small changes can have big effects. A change of 10 parts per billion of certain things in your blood can make the difference between health and sickness.

- Write down the things that:
  - o Make you happy
  - o You do to keep yourself happy
  - o You avoid so you don't feel unhappy
  - o You still want to initiate
  - o Make you unhappy

NOTES

_____

_____

_____

_____

_____

_____

NOTES

_____

_____

_____

_____

_____

_____

_____

_____

_____

_____

_____

_____

Happiness is not a station that you arrive at,

but a manner of travelling.

Anonymous

18.0 Adverse Factors

This book has discussed many topics that can make life happier. What this book also wants to recognize is that there are many things that can adversely affect a person's happiness that are much harder to overcome than through some of the techniques mentioned. These factors include:

- Stress
- Anxiety
- Grief and Loss
- Guilt
- Negative Feelings
- Parental Challenges
- Addiction
- Health Issues
- Abuse
- Relationship Issues
- Past Traumas
- Work Situations
- Depression
- Financial Problems

Some of these challenges may require additional help, such as professional counselling or therapy. Please ensure you have the support you need. If you don't have enough support, consider help lines, associations, religious groups, medical and professional assistance, virtual support and family or friends.

NOTES

19.0 Resilience

Resilience is the ability of a person to either tolerate or bounce back from an adverse event. Why do some people tolerate negative events better than others?

The answer seems to lie in a combination of the personality of the person, their ability to tap into their own strengths and the support systems available to them. Your resilience will be greater if: you do have support, you can identify the things that you can control, and you believe the future will be more positive. Your resilience may be helped if you are also able to tap into your faith. Sometimes taking time to do a favourite activity, such as meditation, physical exercise or another enjoyable activity, will help you recover.

Think about how you have reacted to a past adverse situation in your life. Could you have done something different, thought differently or accessed some external support that would have improved things? Try to focus on happiness in both good times and tough times. Is there an activity or other thing that you could do or change to make the next challenge easier?

The only constant is change, and change happens all the time. When uncomfortable change happens, you will be better prepared for it if you have implemented some of the concepts in this book and kept to your "happiness" practices as best as you can.

20.0 The Happiness Foundation

Your degree of happiness is usually the random result of all the things you do during your life. Having more happiness in life takes some additional effort, planning, and focus. It does not happen by itself. Life is a winding road with many twists and turns, some planned and many unplanned. Take the time to influence the planned road.

So far, the topics that have been discussed have been quite practical in nature. This was done on purpose because they are more easily achievable than working at the emotional level, which is discussed next. The practical suggestions already mentioned will hopefully provide you with a greater degree of happiness – a foundation that you can use if you want to address some emotional issues.

Here is a summary of the bigger topics that were discussed.
- ♥ Exercise
- ♥ Eat good food
- ♥ Make lists
- ♥ Enjoy the road toward achievement
- ♥ Learn from failure
- ♥ Have gratitude
- ♥ Be happy for others
- ♥ Have variety, change the activity
- ♥ Minimize public and interpersonal negativity
- ♥ Put unappreciative people in their own 'Issues Box'
- ♥ Lower expectations
- ♥ Be more forgiving

- ♥ Enjoy the right type of social interaction
- ♥ Learn when to say no
- ♥ Spend a few minutes per day on your happiness goals

Other concepts mentioned in the book to increase happiness can include:

- Smiling more
- Being kind
- Having time for yourself
- Getting enough sleep
- Sticking to your ethics
- Enjoying laughter
- Singing
- Journaling
- Listening or Playing Music
- Enjoying Nature
- Seeing a long view
- Seeing beauty in everything
- Engaging in Art
- Trying Reiki
- Enjoying Religion
- Spending time with a pet
- Using Relaxation techniques

Finally, consider a long-term project to:

- √ Find your passion
- √ Have a five-year plan

Hopefully, some of these ideas have encouraged you to make a positive change in your life toward more happiness. By implementing some of the practical suggestions, you will have improved your 'foundation of happiness', and then that will allow you to address if you want, some emotional factors that may impede or restrict happiness in your life.

NOTES

_____

_____

_____

_____

_____

_____

_____

_____

Don't let praise go you to your head,

and don't let criticism go to your heart.

Rigel Dawson

NOTES

21.0 A Practical Look at Emotions

21.1 General

As previously stated, most of the suggestions so far in this book could be considered quite pragmatic. They allow you to form a 'strong foundation' of happiness in your life. These suggestions also put you in a better place to deal with other difficult factors that may impact your happiness.

If you have implemented some of the items in the previous sections and feel happy, it may be worth giving a brief thought to looking at the emotional component of happiness. Bringing some emotions to the surface and recognizing them, accepting them, dealing with them or loving them will contribute to happiness. Unlike many of the other suggestions in this book, this area takes some real thought, self-reflection and internal observation. Many experts have published excellent books on this topic.

The following short section of suggestions is made with the proviso that they are an engineer's very practical approach to raising your awareness of how emotions can impact your happiness.

21.2 Awareness

Before getting into the topic of emotions, one needs to be aware of oneself, which is actually not very common. Most people are not conscious of how they are seen by other people as a result of their own actions or lack of actions. For example, are you seen as:

- Empathetic
- A talker
- A good listener
- Positive

- Distant
- Loving
- Always late
- Considerate

How you are seen does not necessarily need to impact your happiness unless you are aware of situations that create an unhappy feeling inside you. Are there situations where afterward you feel sad or angry? Was that feeling caused by the other person's behaviours or your own personality? What could you have done to change the outcome of that situation? Does that scenario repeat itself? Does it create an unhappy feeling inside you? Did you make someone else unhappy?

As an exercise, take the time to write one page every night for a week on what you were aware of during the day in your interactions and how you felt.

Recognize your feelings. Perceive your emotions. What should I change? What am I thankful for? What could be different?

21.3 Four Emotions

There are a few opinions on how many emotions there are, but the basic ones are:

o Happiness
o Sadness
o Fear
o Anger

Sadness can be feeling lonely, vulnerable, depressed, guilty, hurt or despair. Angry can be feeling let down, mad, humiliated, aggressive, bitter, frustrated, distant or critical. Fear can include being anxious, doubtful, procrastinating, making excuses, and imagining negative events.

If there are times when you do not feel happy, then why do you feel sad, fearful or angry? Is your negative feeling something that is pervasive, occasional, deep routed or something more recent? It is not the intention of this book to delve into emotional issues in great detail since emotions are a result of a combination of personality and life experiences, and sometimes it is difficult to change one's emotional perspective without considerable effort and, at times, professional assistance. That said, it may be possible to minimize some negative emotions through awareness, reflection, and journaling.

Remember, most of your stress comes

from the way you respond,

not the way your life is.

Adjust your attitude,

and all that extra stress is gone.

Anonymous

21.4 Addressing Anger

According to the English charity 'Mind', anger becomes a problem when:

- you regularly express your anger through unhelpful or destructive behaviour

- your anger is having a negative impact on your overall mental and physical health

- anger becomes your go-to emotion, blocking out your ability to feel other emotions

- you haven't developed healthy ways to express your anger (© Mind. This information is published in full at mind.org.uk)

The following is a 'Happiness' suggestion of how you might address feeling anger at inappropriate times. The same process can be used for sadness or fear. Anger can be either an internal feeling or an external outburst. If you are angry, you are not happy. Try the following process when you feel angrier than the situation warrants. In a journal, write down the following:

(a) What situation made you angry?
(b) How could you have dealt with it in another way?
(c) Make a list of your positive traits.
(d) Make a list of what you are thankful for.

117

(e) Write why you expressed anger – not about the situation but from an internal emotional point of view.

(f) Write statements that get to the feeling under anger. For example, "I am disappointed, not angry." Many times, anger comes as a result of another emotion.

(g) What do you need to do to not feel angry?

Don't rush this process. Take your time to complete parts (a) through (f), and repeat them when you feel angry again. Then work on the things you need to do to feel less angry (g).

Here is an example:

(a) I expressed anger at my wife because I had to drive across the city to pick up a parcel for my son.

(b) I could have been more proactive earlier in the week to inquire about the parcel and arrange a delivery

(c) I am affectionate, a hard worker, ethical, trustworthy, healthy, successful, artistic, and friendly....

(d) I am thankful for my family, health, golf, coffee in the morning, nature, my job, friends, flowers, and ability to write a book.

(e) I was angry because I:
   i. don't express my feelings on a regular basis
   ii. am tired
   iii. am defensive

iv. do too much for other people

    v. want more time for myself

    vi. grew up in a family that did not express emotions

(f) I am:

    i. sad, not angry

    ii. disappointed, not angry

    iii. unhappy, not angry

    iv. down, not angry

    v. overwhelmed, not angry

    vi. able to discuss without anger

After you have done this a few times, review your notes and then write down what you need to do to avoid the anger emotion – either internally or externally.

(g) I need to:

    i. be more aware of my emotions

    ii. write down my emotions in a journal

    iii. discuss my feelings when they happen and not bottle them up

    iv. spend more time exercising

    v. take a minute of awareness when I feel emotions coming and think, "Be calm, stay calm, take five, then discuss."

    vi. realize that things can often be solved through open discussion

See how this process works for you. There are a lot of other techniques that can also be found on the internet or with the assistance of a counsellor.

Hans Schols

NOTES

NOTES

I decide how happy I want to be,

most of the time.

Hans Schols, P. Eng.

22.0 Conclusion

Happiness is not something that one directly pursues but is the result of all the things that you do over time. With the right attitude and approach, you can improve your feeling of happiness in life by taking some additional proactive measures. Life throws challenges at everyone, but if you have a good foundation of happiness, you also will have more resiliency to adapt to new challenges.

Everyone has a gift, a different personality and a life experience, so it is important for you to determine what happiness means to you and how and when you might want to improve it.

This book discusses many different ideas and concepts to improve your happiness, many of which you are probably already doing and some that you hopefully have added to your daily life. Some concepts are quite practical, like exercise or having time alone. Some suggestions are a practical approach to more complex issues, like emotional awareness, which takes more energy and time in order to change a viewpoint, thought process or attitude. Enjoy the continued journey of discovery, failure and success by trying something new. By doing this, your neurotransmitters and hormones will naturally increase, as will your happiness.

Be kind to yourself as you continue on your journey of improving your own feeling of happiness. Do more research on your own to see what works for you in terms of mental, physical, emotional and social health.

The physical and mental body is an amazing piece of machinery that responds to change – whether it is the strength to walk further or the ability to be more positive because you are taking on a new project, staying away from negative news, finding beauty in every day or whatever other changes you have decided to implement!

An Engineer's Poem on Happiness

Smile, be kind and eat well
And exercise before the bell
Be ethical and moral with gratitude
Enjoy nature, music and solitude

Try to avoid the negatives
Whether media, friends or relatives
And if a person says something hostile
Realize it's just their own crazy lifestyle

Have a schedule, have a goal
Focus on values in your heart and soul
Happiness does not have a secret code
Why not travel this wonderful road?

Hans Schols, P. Eng.

NOTES

Table of Contents

23.0 Appendix

Here are a few other ideas that make for interesting reading if you wish to research the topic.

A1   *The Philosophy of Stoicism*

A2   *The Seven Teachings of the Anishinaabe*

A3   *Books on Personal Well-Being by Dr. Rick Hanson*

A4   *Books on Stress by Dr. David Posen*

A5   *The Japanese Concept of Ikigai*

A6   *The Dalai Lama Eight Pillars of Joy*

A1 Stoicism

Stoicism is a school of philosophy that hails from ancient Greece and Rome in the early parts of the third century BCE. It is a philosophy of life that maximizes positive emotions, reduces negative emotions and helps individuals hone their virtues of character. The four virtues of stoicism are:

- Courage – bravery
- Justice - fairness
- Temperance - restraint
- Wisdom – understanding/insight

Some of the philosophies of stoicism are:

- Recognize what you can and cannot control.
- You determine your reaction to a crisis.
- Ignore people dominated by their own negative emotions.
- Master yourself and aim to be virtuous.
- Learn to move on.

There are many books and articles available on this topic.

A2 The Seven Teachings of the Anishinaabe

The Anishinaabe are a group of culturally related indigenous peoples present in the Great Lakes region of Canada and the United States. They include the Ojibwe, Odawa, Potawatomi, Mississaugas, Nipissing and Algonquin peoples. The Seven Teachings are the guiding principles in the collaboration toward the restoration of the cultural values, beliefs, and practices that were forbidden.

It is worth reading about the seven teachings:

Wisdom

Love

Respect

Bravery

Honesty

Humility

Truth

It is also insightful to read the Haudenosaunee Thanksgiving Address and their gratitude to the Earth Mother.

A3 Books on Well Being by Dr. Rick Hanson

Dr. Hanson is a psychologist who has written and taught about the essential inner skills of personal well-being, psychological growth, and contemplative practice – as well as about relationships, family life, and raising children. His books include:

- o Neurodharma: Experience the heights of human potential with seven practices grounded in new science and ancient teachings.

- o Resilient: Develop twelve key inner strengths for lasting well-being in a changing world.

- o Hardwiring Happiness: Beat the brain's negativity bias with four steps using positive neuroplasticity for lasting contentment, calm, and confidence.

- o Buddha's Brain: Change your brain and your life with the practical neuroscience of happiness, love, and wisdom.

- o Just One Thing: 52 short practices for peace of mind, inner strength, and lasting contentment.

A4 Books on Stress by Dr. David Posen

Dr. David Posen is a medical doctor who is an author, trainer, speaker and authority on stress management. His books include:

o <u>Authenticity</u>: A Guide to Living in Harmony with Your True Self

o <u>Is Work Killing You</u>: A Doctor's Prescription for Treating Workplace Stress

o <u>Always Change a Losing Game</u>: Winning Strategies for Work, Home and Health

o <u>The Little Book of Stress Relief</u>

A5 Ikigai

The Oxford English Dictionary defines the Japanese concept of ikigai as "a motivating force; something or someone that gives a person a sense of purpose or a reason for living". More generally, it may refer to something that brings pleasure or fulfilment.

Ikigai is not about what the world needs from you. Ikigai lies in the realm of community, family, friendships and in the roles you fulfill. When you pursue your ikigai, you are not out to save the world. It is more about connecting with and helping the people who give meaning to your life - your family, friends, co-workers and community.

You don't have to be good at something to find your ikigai. Ikigai can be a very simple daily ritual or the practice of a new hobby. Ikigai is more about growth rather than mastery. Ikigai can be something you love or are passionate about, but you can find ikigai in areas of your life you would least expect. Ikigai is more about living your values and finding meaning and purpose in daily living, regardless of what constraints you may have. The areas discussed in ikigai include:

- Passion
- Purpose
- Satisfaction
- Fulfillment
- Calling
- True Self
- Values

- Good for society
- Fulfilment, longevity and happiness
- Reason for being
- Nothing exists in a vacuum

A6 Eight Pillars of Joy by the Dalai Lama

The Dalai Lama's perspective also provides insightful reading.

1. Perspective
2. Humility
3. Humour
4. Acceptance
5. Forgiveness
6. Gratitude
7. Compassion
8. Generosity

About The Author

Hans Schols is happy living life as a husband and father, as well as an entrepreneur launching a hi-tech insurance platform with lots of challenges, a professional engineer focused on practical methodologies, an amateur photographer trying to create new expressions, and an observer of how people react to positive and negative experiences. Previously Hans was also a corporate leader motivating people in companies across three continents and an athlete competing at the international level.

He has had successes and failures, been happy and unhappy and has learned and relearned some life lessons many times. Hans loves learning, solving both technical problems and creating positive experiences that allow individuals to feel a sense of accomplishment and happiness. Interestingly, during the creation of this book, he learned more about himself and worked through a few issues to be a happier person. Hans enjoys spending time with his family and friends in both Canada and the United States and working with colleagues in Australia.

Thanks for reading this book.

**If you have any comments,
please send them to**

happiness@glenelgintl.com

NOTES

To the optimist, the glass is half full.

To the pessimist, the glass is half empty.

*To the engineer, the glass is twice as
big as it needs to be.*

Anonymous

NOTES

Engineers like to solve problems.

If there are no problems handily available,

they will create their own problems.

Scott Adams

NOTES

Made in United States
North Haven, CT
12 March 2023

33963044R00083